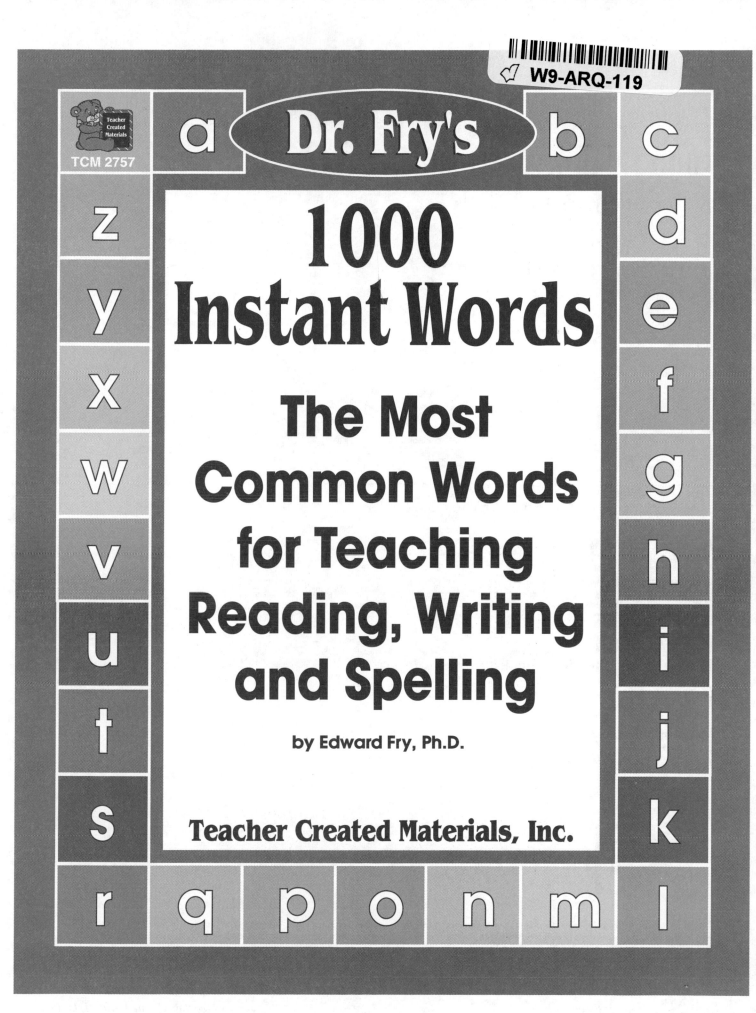

TCM 2757

Teacher Created Materials

a b c d e f g h i j k l m n o p q r s t u v w x y z

Dr. Fry's
1000 Instant Words

The Most Common Words for Teaching Reading, Writing and Spelling

by Edward Fry, Ph.D.

Teacher Created Materials, Inc.

1000 Instant Words

by Edward Fry, Ph.D.

Teacher Created Materials, Inc.
6421 Industry Way
Westminster, CA 92683
www.teachercreated.com
ISBN-1-57690-757-0

©1999 by Edward Fry
Laguna Beach Educational Books

©2000 Revised by Teacher Created Materials, Inc.
Reprinted, 2003

Made in U.S.A.

Table of Contents

Introduction

In the English language, there are a number of words that have been scientifically determined to be the most commonly used words in the language. These high-frequency words are referred to as "Instant Words" because they are words that should be recognized instantly by readers. *1000 Instant Words* contains a list of the 1000 most commonly used words in the English language and is a basic tool for reading and writing teachers, curriculum developers, literacy tutors, authors of children's books, and researchers.

Beginning readers, who for now we will define as those whose reading ability ranges from none to upper fifth grade, need to master a high-frequency vocabulary such as the Instant Words. In fact, they need to be able to read the first 300 Instant Words without a moment's hesitation because these 300 words make up 65% of all written material! Over half of every newspaper article, textbook, children's story, and novel is composed of just these 300 words! These are words that come up over and over again—words like *and*, *of*, and *the*. It is difficult to write any sentence without using several of the first 300 Instant Words.

Another reason for learning the Instant Words is that some of these often-used words do not follow regular phonics rules very well. For example, how do you sound out *of* or *said*? The answer is that beginning readers need to learn these words as "sight" words, and beginning readers also need to learn to spell these common words.

The core of this book is 1000 Instant Words ranked in order of frequency (i.e., the most common words listed first). These 1000 words are arranged in groups of five words to indicate to the teacher that only a few should be taught at one time. This "rank order" is also the suggested order in which beginning readers or writers normally learn new basic words. (Of course, children and adults learn many other subject words, like names and subject matter words, too.)

This list of 1000 Instant Words is followed by the same words arranged in alphabetical order (in case you want to look up the position of any word). The list is based on the American Heritage five-million word count but has a different ranking because variant word forms were combined and subsequently re-ranked.

The next section tells how to test your student(s) so that you can start teaching the Instant Words at an appropriate place. This will aid you in selecting words to teach to children or adults who have some, but not very complete, reading or writing ability.

Following that are some suggestions on how to teach the Instant Words with reading practice, flash cards, games, and spelling lessons.

Finally, there is a section with 100 Picture Nouns, which are nouns illustrated by pictures. These are a useful addition to the Instant Words because they can be used to help students write more meaningful sentences or read useful words that might not occur in the 1000 Instant Words. The picture nouns are also effective for students who learn reading and writing best through the use of concrete or easily-visualized words.

Rank Order 1–30

1–5

the
of
and
a
to

16–20

as
with
his
they
I

6–10

in
is
you
that
it

21–25

at
be
this
have
from

11–15

he
was
for
on
are

26–30

or
one
had
by
word

Rank Order 31–60

31–35

but
not
what
all
were

46–50

she
do
how
their
if

36–40

we
when
your
can
said

51–55

will
up
other
about
out

41–45

there
use
an
each
which

56–60

many
then
them
these
so

Rank Order 61–90

61–65

some
her
would
make
like

76–80

number
no
way
could
people

66–70

him
into
time
has
look

81–85

my
than
first
water
been

71–75

two
more
write
go
see

86–90

call
who
oil
now
find

Rank Order 91–120

91–95

long
down
day
did
get

96–100

come
made
may
part
over

101–105

new
sound
take
only
little

106–110

work
know
place
year
live

111–115

me
back
give
most
very

116–120

after
thing
our
just
name

Rank Order 121–150

121–125

good
sentence
man
think
say

136–140

old
any
same
tell
boy

126–130

great
where
help
through
much

141–145

follow
came
want
show
also

131–135

before
line
right
too
mean

146–150

around
farm
three
small
set

Rank Order 151–180

151–155

put
end
does
another
well

166–170

went
men
read
need
land

156–160

large
must
big
even
such

171–175

different
home
us
move
try

161–165

because
turn
here
why
ask

176–180

kind
hand
picture
again
change

Rank Order 181–210

181–185

off
play
spell
air
away

196–200

learn
should
America
world
high

186–190

animal
house
point
page
letter

201–205

every
near
add
food
between

191–195

mother
answer
found
study
still

206–210

own
below
country
plant
last

Rank Order 211–240

211–215

school
father
keep
tree
never

226–230

left
don't
few
while
along

216–220

start
city
earth
eye
light

231–235

might
close
something
seem
next

221–225

thought
head
under
story
saw

236–240

hard
open
example
begin
life

Rank Order 241–270

241–245

always
those
both
paper
together

256–260

mile
night
walk
white
sea

246–250

got
group
often
run
important

261–265

began
grow
took
river
four

251–255

until
children
side
feet
car

266–270

carry
state
once
book
hear

Rank Order 271–300

271–275

stop
without
second
late
miss

286–290

above
girl
sometimes
mountain
cut

276–280

idea
enough
eat
face
watch

291–295

young
talk
soon
list
song

281–285

far
Indian
real
almost
let

296–300

being
leave
family
it's
afternoon

Rank Order 301–330

301–305

body
music
color
stand
sun

306–310

questions
fish
area
mark
dog

311–315

horse
birds
problem
complete
room

316–320

knew
since
ever
piece
told

321–325

usually
didn't
friends
easy
heard

326–330

order
red
door
sure
become

331–335

top
ship
across
today
during

346–350

measure
remember
early
waves
reached

336–340

short
better
best
however
low

351–355

listen
wind
rock
space
covered

341–345

hours
black
products
happened
whole

356–360

fast
several
hold
himself
toward

361–365

five
step
morning
passed
vowel

376–380

farm
pulled
draw
voice
seen

366–370

true
hundred
against
pattern
numeral

381–385

cold
cried
plan
notice
south

371–375

table
north
slowly
money
map

386–390

sing
war
ground
fall
king

391–395

town
I'll
unit
figure
certain

396–400

field
travel
wood
fire
upon

401–405

done
English
road
half
ten

406–410

fly
gave
box
finally
wait

411–415

correct
oh
quickly
person
became

416–420

shown
minutes
strong
verb
stars

421–425

front
feel
fact
inches
street

436–440

rest
carefully
scientists
inside
wheels

426–430

decided
contain
course
surface
produce

441–445

stay
green
known
island
week

431–435

building
ocean
class
note
nothing

446–450

less
machine
base
ago
stood

Rank Order 451–480

451–455

plane
system
behind
ran
round

466–470

though
language
shape
deep
thousands

456–460

boat
game
force
brought
understand

471–475

yes
clear
equation
yet
government

461–465

warm
common
bring
explain
dry

476–480

filled
heat
full
hot
check

481–485

object
am
rule
among
noun

486–490

power
cannot
able
six
size

491–495

dark
ball
material
special
heavy

496–500

fine
pair
circle
include
built

501–505

can't
matter
square
syllables
perhaps

506–510

bill
felt
suddenly
test
direction

511–515

center
farmers
ready
anything
divided

516–520

general
energy
subject
Europe
moon

521–525

region
return
believe
dance
members

526–530

picked
simple
cells
paint
mind

531–535

love
cause
rain
exercise
eggs

536–540

train
blue
wish
drop
developed

541–545

window
difference
distance
heart
sit

546–550

sum
summer
wall
forest
probably

551–555

legs
sat
main
winter
wide

556–560

written
length
reason
kept
interest

561–565

arms
brother
race
present
beautiful

566–570

store
job
edge
past
sign

Rank Order 571–600

571–575

record
finished
discovered
wild
happy

586–590

meet
third
months
paragraph
raised

576–580

beside
gone
sky
glass
million

591–595

represent
soft
whether
clothes
flowers

581–585

west
lay
weather
root
instruments

596–600

shall
teacher
held
describe
drive

601–605

cross
speak
solve
appear
metal

606–610

son
either
ice
sleep
village

611–615

factors
result
jumped
snow
ride

616–620

care
floor
hill
pushed
baby

621–625

buy
century
outside
everything
tall

626–630

already
instead
phrase
soil
bed

631–635

copy
free
hope
spring
case

646–650

section
lake
consonant
within
dictionary

636–640

laughed
nation
quite
type
themselves

651–655

hair
age
amount
scale
pounds

641–645

temperature
bright
lead
everyone
method

656–660

although
per
broken
moment
tiny

Rank Order 661–690

661–665

possible
gold
milk
quiet
natural

666–670

lot
stone
act
build
middle

671–675

speed
count
cat
someone
sail

676–680

rolled
bear
wonder
smiled
angle

681–685

fraction
Africa
killed
melody
bottom

686–690

trip
hole
poor
let's
fight

691–695

surprise
French
died
beat
exactly

706–710

shouted
continued
itself
else
plains

696–700

remain
dress
iron
couldn't
fingers

711–715

gas
England
burning
design
joined

701–705

row
least
catch
climbed
wrote

716–720

foot
law
ears
grass
you're

Rank Order 721–750

721–725

grew
skin
valley
cents
key

726–730

president
brown
trouble
cool
cloud

731–735

lost
sent
symbols
wear
bad

736–740

save
experiment
engine
alone
drawing

741–745

east
pay
single
touch
information

746–750

express
mouth
yard
equal
decimal

751–755

yourself
control
practice
report
straight

766–770

wire
choose
clean
visit
bit

756–760

rise
statement
stick
party
seeds

771–775

whose
received
garden
please
strange

761–765

suppose
woman
coast
bank
period

776–780

caught
fell
team
God
captain

781–785

direct
ring
serve
child
desert

796–800

lady
students
human
art
feeling

786–790

increase
history
cost
maybe
business

801–805

supply
corner
electric
insects
crops

791–795

separate
break
uncle
hunting
flow

806–810

tone
hit
sand
doctor
provide

Rank Order 811–840

811–815

thus
won't
cook
bones
tail

816–820

board
modern
compound
mine
wasn't

821–825

fit
addition
belong
safe
soldiers

826–830

guess
silent
trade
rather
compare

831–835

crowd
poem
enjoy
elements
indicate

836-840

except
expect
flat
seven
interesting

841–845

sense
string
blow
famous
value

856–860

fun
loud
consider
suggested
thin

846–850

wings
movement
pole
exciting
branches

861–865

position
entered
fruit
tied
rich

851–855

thick
blood
lie
spot
bell

866–870

dollars
send
sight
chief
Japanese

Rank Order 871–900

871–875

stream
planets
rhythm
eight
science

886–890

property
particular
swim
terms
current

876–880

major
observe
tube
necessary
weight

891–895

park
sell
shoulder
industry
wash

881–885

meat
lifted
process
army
hat

896–900

block
spread
cattle
wife
sharp

Rank Order 901–930

901–905

company
radio
we'll
action
capital

916–920

chance
born
level
triangle
molecules

906–910

factories
settled
yellow
isn't
southern

921–925

France
repeated
column
western
church

911–915

truck
fair
printed
wouldn't
ahead

926–930

sister
oxygen
plural
various
agreed

Rank Order 931–960

931–935

opposite
wrong
chart
prepared
pretty

936–940

solution
fresh
shop
suffix
especially

941–945

shoes
actually
nose
afraid
dead

946–950

sugar
adjective
fig
office
huge

951–955

gun
similar
death
score
forward

956–960

stretched
experienced
rose
allow
fear

Rank Order 961–990

961–965

workers
Washington
Greek
women
bought

976–980

total
deal
determine
evening
nor

966–970

led
march
northern
create
British

981–985

rope
cotton
apple
details
entire

971–975

difficult
match
win
doesn't
steel

986–990

corn
substances
smell
tools
conditions

Rank Order 991–1000

991–995

cows

track

arrived

located

sir

996–1000

seat

division

effect

underline

view

Testing the Instant Words

Children and adults who are just learning or who have failed to learn to read properly from regular instruction frequently have a very irregular reading vocabulary. They may know some relatively uncommon words but may not know some of the words that appear most frequently.

Older basic reading textbooks have their own graded list built into the series, but perhaps your student has followed no basic text series or has learned only part of the list. If so, you must find out the level of each student's knowledge and skills.

To do this with an individual student is easy. Use the "Instant Word Test" (pages 41 and 42), or simply ask the student to read aloud from each column of the Instant Words. Then stop and teach the words he doesn't know.

If you work with groups, a way of diagnosing word knowledge for beginning readers is to make a recognition test. Photocopy a group of Instant Words, four words per line with each line numbered. Give each student a sheet with the words on it and then say, "On line 1 put an *X* on the word *you*, on line 2 put an *X* on the word *that*," and so on.

By correcting the tests, you can easily sort the pupils into groups by ability. Incidentally, save the tests and use them for the students to study from or to review the words.

If you don't want to use this survey test, just have your student read every Instant Word (pages 5–38) but not all at once. Use a page or part of a page for each lesson until you have accumulated enough unknown words for the day's lesson.

Directions for the Instant Word Test

The "Instant Word Test" is located on the next page. Ask the pupil to read each word aloud slowly. The examiner should use a copy of the "Instant Word Test" for scoring. Place an X next to each word read incorrectly or omitted. Although you should allow for dialect differences, accept only meaningful pronunciations. Do not give any assistance. If a pupil does not know a word after five seconds, tell him to go on to the next word.

Discontinue the test when the student misses five words, not necessarily in consecutive order. Find the last correct word before the fifth error, and multiply its position number by 15. This will give you the student's approximate instructional placement.

Because it is not standardized, this test does not yield a grade-level score, but it can be used to determine where to begin working with a student on the 1000 Instant Words. Do not use this test for teaching; use the complete list of Instant Words.

Instant Word Test

Student's Name_____

Examiner_____

Date _____ Class _____

Directions: The student reads aloud from one copy, and the examiner marks another copy. Stop after the student misses any five words, and note the position number of the last correct word. Do not help the student. If the student makes an error or hesitates for five seconds, say, "Try the next word."

Scoring: Multiply the position number of the last correct word (before the fifth word missed) by 15, which will result in the student's approximate placement in the 1000 Instant Words.

(   ) position number of last correct word before the fifth word missed

   x   15

(   ) approximate placement in the 1000 Instant Words

For example, if the last correct word was 10, then 10 x 15 = 150, which is the student's score. As a result, you would then begin teaching the Instant Words with word 151.

Test for the First 300 Words

(approximately every 15th word in the first 300 words)

1. are	11. why
2. but	12. again
3. which	13. study
4. so	14. last
5. see	15. story
6. now	16. beginning
7. only	17. feet
8. just	18. book
9. too	19. almost
10. small	20. family

Instant Word Test *(cont.)*

Test for the Second 300 Words
(approximately every 15th word in the second 300 words)

21. room	31. bring
22. become	32. check
23. whole	33. heavy
24. toward	34. direction
25. map	35. picked
26. king	36. window
27. certain	37. wide
28. stars	38. sign
29. nothing	39. root
30. stood	40. describe

Test for the Next 400 Words
(approximately every 15th word in the next 400 words)

41. ride	54. provide
42. bed	55. guess
43. lake	56. interesting
44. tiny	57. bell
45. sail	58. chief
46. fight	59. army
47. wrote	60. sharp
48. grew	61. chance
49. save	62. agreed
50. equal	63. dead
51. choose	64. fear
52. direct	65. total
53. flow	66. conditions

Teaching the
Instant Words

Since a high percentage of all reading material is composed of relatively few words, learning to read would appear to be a task that is fairly easy. If 300 words will do such a large percentage of the job, why not begin with just these words, teach them quickly, and get it over with at once? The trouble is that it is not that easy.

Experience has shown that, normally, mastery of the first 300 Instant Words (or of any basic vocabulary list of this size for that matter) could be expected to take nearly three years for primary children. An average student in an average school situation learns most of the first 100 words toward the end of the first year. The second hundred words are added during the second year. It is not until some time in the third year that all 300 words are really mastered and used as a part of the student's own reading vocabulary. This is not to deny that second and third graders can "read" many more words than the 300 Instant Words. They can also read many proper nouns and some subject words related to the type of material to which they have been exposed.

One can expect to decrease the learning time required in the case of older students, illiterate adults, and students in upper elementary and secondary remedial reading classes. Still, their learning of the first 300 Instant Words is found to closely parallel their attained reading ability level. For example, a person who can just manage to read upper second-grade material barely knows most of the first 200 Instant Words.

Of the list of 1000 Instant Words given in this book, make sure that your students know most of the first 300 Instant Words. The rest of the 1000 Instant Words are for reading and spelling lessons with students of fourth- and fifth-grade ability.

Methods for teaching the Instant Words vary with the teacher, the pupil, and the educational situation. Any method that works is a good method. We suggest easy reading practice, flash cards, card games, and spelling lessons augmented by lavish praise, encouragement, friendly competition, or a play-therapy climate. The pupil learns to read words in books, on flash cards, in his own compositions, or off wall charts. Teach him alone and in large groups, in the classroom or out under the trees; but all the while, constantly teach three things by word and deed:

1. We care about you.

2. We want you to read.

3. These Instant Words are important.

Note that the Instant Words are in groups of five. This is a reminder to only teach a few words at a time. Some students can learn only two or three words per week, and others can master 20. Both need frequent review. Here are some specific methods to help teach the Instant Words.

Teaching the
Instant Words *(cont.)*

Easy Reading Practice

Easy reading practice is one of the best ways of teaching the Instant Words. "Easy reading" is reading that is a grade or two below where the student "can" (with help or hesitancy) read. For a student who can read on the second-grade level, easy reading is reading first-grade level materials. For a student who can read at a sixth-grade level, easy reading is at the fourth- or fifth-grade level. (It is no accident that most popular novels are written at about the eighth-grade difficulty level although most book buyers are at least high school graduates.)

In his book *Foundations of Reading Instruction* (American Book Company, 1957), E.A. Betts defined easy reading material as printed matter in which a student can pronounce 99 percent of the words. Another Betts' rule-of-thumb was that when the student averages less than one mistake for every 20 words, the material is "easy" for him.

Easy reading practice is especially beneficial because the material is certain to contain the Instant Words, and a student who barely knows these words gets practice in recognizing them. Easy reading practice helps a student to learn to apply context clues. It also gives the student a feeling of success and encourages him to try to learn more.

Flash Cards

Many teachers, tutors, and parents use flash cards to help teach sight word reading. (See the inside back cover for information about ordering sets of ready-made flash cards.) A flash card is simply a card with a word written on it. The word is written in bold print using a marker or dark crayon. Usually the print is in lowercase letters. If the upper right-hand corner is cut off, the printed word will always be right side up and facing you when the cards are restacked.

A traditional way to teach using flash cards is to take a small number of words, such as five Instant Words. Tell the student each word and discuss it a little, perhaps using it in an oral sentence. Next, mix up the cards and "flash" them while the student tries to quickly call out the word. If incorrect, tell him the word; don't use phonics at this point. Mix up the words and flash them to the student again. After the student knows all the words, put them away and review them again during the next lesson, helping the student with any missed words.

Teaching the Instant Words *(cont.)*

Flash Cards *(cont.)*

One of the nice things about flash cards is that they make great review lessons, and students often require lots of review of these words. Just because students have mastered the list one day, don't be surprised if they don't remember all the words next week. This is why review and more practice are needed. Incidentally, don't blame the student for forgetting. Instead, offer praise for any words he does remember and then patiently teach the missed words. Remember that everyone needs repetition in learning new things, whether it's people's names or a new subject being studied.

Another way that flash cards can be used is to display them for referral at other times during the day. Teachers might line them up on the chalkboard, parents might stick them on the refrigerator, and/or tutors might hand a small stack to the student to take home for practice.

Flash cards can also be used as sentence builders. Put two, three, or more flash cards in order so that they make a phrase or a sentence. You can even make some interesting sentences using "rebuses." A rebus is simply a picture used instead of a word. Can you read the following rebus? (It says, "The boy hit the dog.")

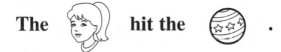

You can use flash cards with small groups, too. The teacher flashes the word as quickly as possible. The student who says the word first gets to hold the card. The point of the game is to see who gets the most cards. Give each student a turn at recognizing the word. When he misses, the next student gets a turn.

A student can also work alone with a small pack of flash cards, separating them into two piles: the cards he knows and those he does not know. When he is finished, a teacher or more advanced student checks on the "know" pile and then helps him with the "don't know" pile.

You can make your own flash cards on blank calling cards (obtained from a printer or office supply store), on 3" x 5" (8 cm x 13 cm) cards, on scraps of paper, or on a computer. You can copy the whole list or just make cards for words the student missed when reading down the list. A student can even make his own flash cards.

Just remember not to teach too many words at once. Keep the student's success rate high!

Teaching the Instant Words *(cont.)*

Bingo Game

Bingo is an excellent game for teaching Instant Words to groups, but it is equally useful for small groups or even a single student. Twenty-five words can be placed on a card (five rows and five columns) in random order with a card for as many students as are playing. The teacher calls off the words in random order or draws the word cards out of a hat or container. Markers can be small squares of cardboard, beans, or anything handy. The first student to complete a row, column, or diagonal line wins.

Oftentimes, even though there has been a winner, the students like to play until their entire cards are filled and every word is covered. If played until the card is filled, the teacher can sometimes spot the poor readers by the number of uncovered words. In a teaching situation where some of the students do not know all the words, effective instruction can ensue by having the teacher show the card or write the word on the board after saying it. This gives poor readers an equal chance at winning, which is always desirable.

Note that by making five rows and five columns, one set of 25 Instant Words will fit on a card. For young children or beginning readers, you can make bingo cards with just nine words (three rows and three columns).

Remember that each player must have a card with the same words, but arranged in a different order.

Sample Bingo Card

the	of	it	with	at
a	can	on	are	this
is	will	you	to	and
your	that	we	as	but
be	in	not	for	have

Teaching the Instant Words *(cont.)*

Pairs Game

Another game played with great success is called Pairs. Pairs is played like Go Fish; only two cards are needed to make a book or pair. Create the card deck with groups of 25 Instant Words; two cards for each word make a 50-card deck. Make the decks for the level of words your students need to learn, and let students help make the decks.

Two to five persons may play. Five cards are dealt to each player, and the remainder of the deck is placed in the center of the table. The object of the game is to get as many pairs as possible. There are only two of each matching Instant Word cards in the deck.

The player to the right of the dealer asks any other player if he has a specific card. For example, "Do you have an *and*?" The player asking must have the mate (in this example, the other *and* card) in his hand. The player who is asked must give up the card if he has it. If the first player does not get the card he asked for, he draws one card from the pile. If the player succeeds in getting the card asked for, either from another player or from the pile, he gets another turn. As soon as the player gets a pair, he puts it down in front of him.

If a player is not able to get a matching pair, then the next player gets a turn at asking for a card. The player with the most pairs at the end of the game wins.

If the player doing the asking does not know how to read the word on the card, he may show the card and ask any of the other players for help. If the player who is asked for a card does not know how to read that word, he may ask to see the card being requested or ask someone not playing to look at his hand.

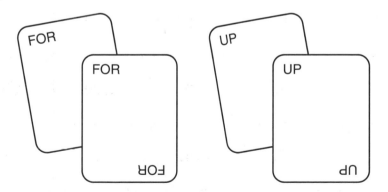

Make two cards for each word in a Pairs game deck.

The students should know some but not all of the words used in a particular deck. They should have help in playing until they know almost all the words and can get along by themselves. They can usually accomplish this quite rapidly as the game is highly motivating.

Teaching the
Instant Words *(cont.)*

Pairs Game *(cont.)*

The students should play the game on several different occasions until they can call out all the words instantly. They should then move to a more difficult deck.

Occasionally, it is good to review easy words already mastered, just for fun. In general, instructional games should follow the same rules as those used in the selection of instructional reading material—not too easy and not too hard.

Concentration

The Pairs decks can also be used to play a Concentration game. Take a deck of 50 cards and place them facedown, spread out in rows on a table in mixed-up order. One to four students can play. The first player turns over any two cards. If they are not a pair, then they must be put back in the same place, facedown, and the next player takes a turn. The trick is to remember the location of cards so one can make a pair with each two cards turned up. The student should read aloud each card turned over. If a player doesn't know how to read the card, another player can help him. The player with the most pairs at the end of the game is the winner.

Spelling

The Instant Words may also be used for spelling lessons, particularly those words which the students have trouble learning to read. The Instant Words are just as important for writing as they are for reading since students can't write a story without using some of the Instant Words.

A Spelling Teaching Method for Teachers

1. **Use the Test-Study Method.** For example, give a trial spelling test on Monday. However, don't give too many words. Five to 10 words for a beginner (first-grade level) and 20 words for grade levels 2–6 are appropriate.

2. **Have the students correct their own papers.** Make sure they write all the words they spelled incorrectly. During the first few weeks, you should check their papers to see that they have both found the words they misspelled and spelled them correctly.

3. **Have the students carefully study the words that they missed,** paying careful attention to the incorrect or missing letters, perhaps by circling the incorrect letter(s) and writing the word correctly from memory several times. (See the "5-Step Spelling Word Study Method for Students" on the following page.)

4. **Give a second spelling test on Wednesday.** Every student who gets 100% (or perhaps 90%) will not have to take the test again on Friday. They can read or write stories during the test instead.

5. **Give a final test on Friday** for only those students who did not do well on Wednesday's test. They should study again, but only the words and letter(s) they missed. You can help them by pointing out phonics, syllabication, spelling patterns, suffix principles, or irregularities.

6. **Each student can keep a chart of final scores** achieved on their final spelling test (Wednesday or Friday).

For more information on teaching spelling, see *Spelling Book: Words Most Needed Plus Phonics for Grades 1-6* (TCM 2750), listed on the inside back cover. This book contains 195 weekly spelling lessons, covering grades 1-6.

Spelling *(cont.)*

5-Step
Spelling Word Study Method
for Students

1. **Look** at the whole word carefully.

2. **Say** the word aloud to yourself.

3. **Spell** the word. Say each letter to yourself.

4. **Write** the word from memory. Cover the word and write it.

5. **Check** your written word against the correct spelling. Circle errors, and repeat steps 4 and 5.

Picture Nouns

"Picture nouns" are nouns illustrated by pictures. They are also words that students need when writing stories. Since the Instant Words do not have many "subject words," or words that tell about the content, the 100 picture nouns (listed on pages 52-61) are intended to supplement the Instant Words. Most of the games and techniques used in teaching the Instant Words can also be used with the picture nouns.

The picture nouns can be taught along with the Instant Words, a group of five at a time. They are particularly useful on flash cards as sentence builders. Make a set of flash cards for the number of words you want to teach. Put the printed word on one side and the picture on the other side. The picture side of the card can be used as a rebus, or a picture that represents a word in a sentence.

 **car**

 **boat**

Picture nouns can also be used to help develop thinking skills. Take two or more groups of five picture nouns, mix them up, and have the student sort them into piles that belong together. It makes the student think about how the words are related and also gives him practice at reading the words. (See the inside back cover for information about ordering sets of ready-made flash cards.)

The picture nouns can be used as self-teaching lessons, too. Give the student a stack of cards with the word side up. The student tries to read the word and then turns the card over to look at the picture. The student gets immediate feedback whether or not he was able to correctly read the word.

Picture Nouns: Groups 1 and 2

Group 1

boy

girl

man

woman

baby

Group 2

ball

doll

train

game

toy

Picture Nouns: Groups 3 and 4

Group 3

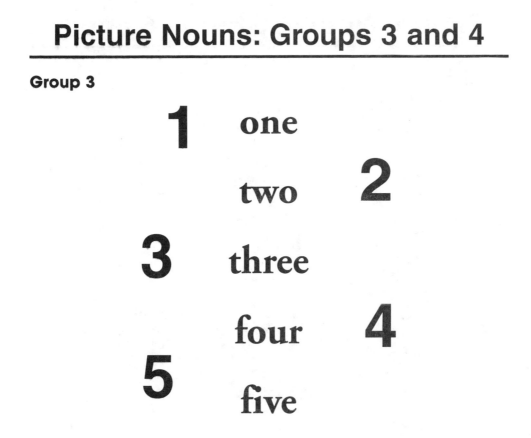

1   one

two   2

3   three

four   4

5   five

Group 4

shirt

pants

dress

shoes

hat

Picture Nouns: Groups 5 and 6

Group 5

cat

dog

bird

fish

rabbit

Group 6

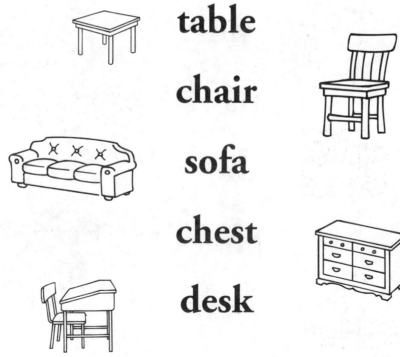

table

chair

sofa

chest

desk

Picture Nouns: Groups 7 and 8

Group 7

cup

plate

bowl

fork

spoon

Group 8

car

truck

bus

plane

boat

Picture Nouns: Groups 9 and 10

Group 9

bread

meat

soup

apple

cereal

Group 10

water

milk

juice

soda

malt

Picture Nouns: Groups 11 and 12

Group 11

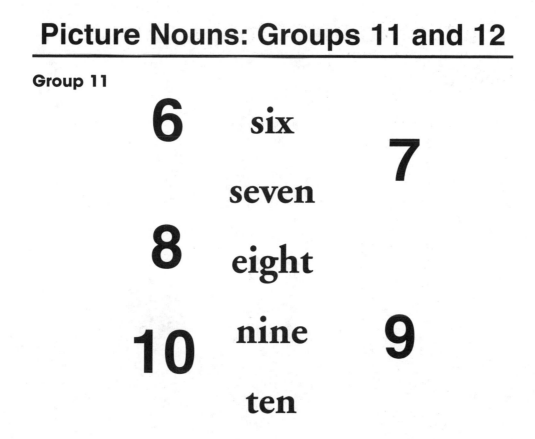

6   six

7

seven

8   eight

nine   9

10

ten

Group 12

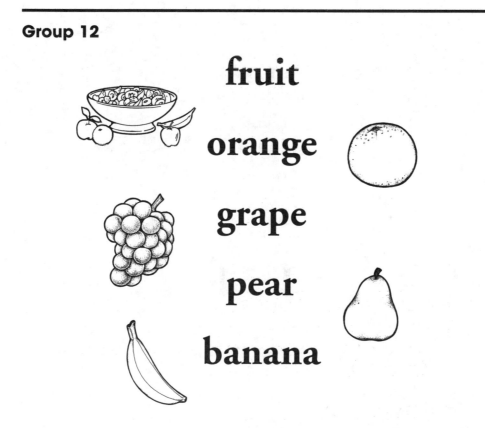

fruit

orange

grape

pear

banana

Picture Nouns: Groups 13 and 14

Group 13

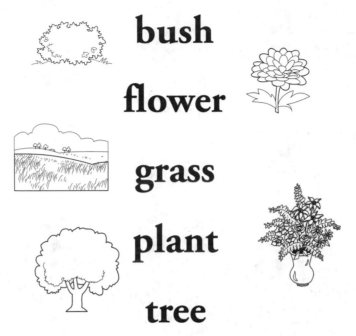

bush

flower

grass

plant

tree

Group 14

sun

moon

star

cloud

rain

Picture Nouns: Groups 15 and 16

Group 15

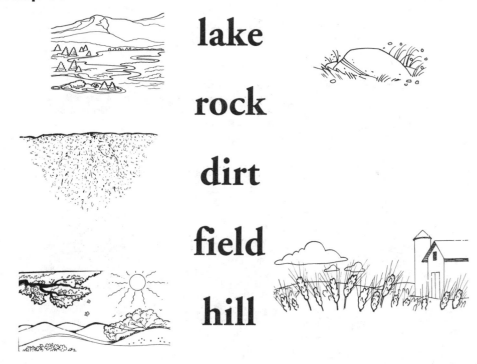

lake

rock

dirt

field

hill

Group 16

horse

cow

pig

chicken

duck

Picture Nouns: Groups 17 and 18

Group 17

 farmer

policeman

 cook

doctor

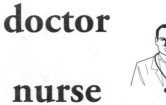 nurse

---

Group 18

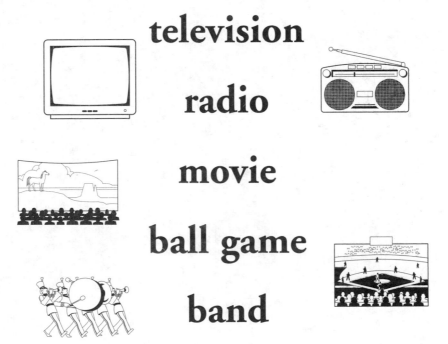

television

radio

movie

ball game

band

Picture Nouns: Groups 19 and 20

Group 19

pen

pencil

crayon

chalk

computer

Group 20

book

newspaper

magazine

sign

letter

Alphabetical Order: A-FOR

Note: Numbers indicate rank order.

Word	#	Word	#	Word	#	Word	#	Word	#
a	4	because	161	catch	703	day	93	equal	749
able	488	become	330	cattle	898	dead	945	equation	473
about	54	bed	630	caught	776	deal	977	especially	940
above	286	been	85	cause	532	death	953	Europe	519
across	333	before	131	cells	528	decided	426	even	159
act	668	began	261	center	511	decimal	750	evening	979
action	904	begin	239	cents	724	deep	469	ever	318
actually	942	behind	453	century	622	describe	599	every	201
add	203	being	296	certain	395	desert	785	everyone	644
addition	822	believe	523	chance	916	design	714	everything	624
adjective	947	bell	855	change	180	details	984	exactly	695
afraid	944	belong	823	chart	933	determine	978	example	238
Africa	682	below	207	check	480	developed	540	except	836
after	116	beside	576	chief	869	dictionary	650	exciting	849
afternoon	300	best	338	child	784	did	94	exercise	534
again	179	better	337	children	252	didn't	322	expect	837
against	368	between	205	choose	767	died	693	experience	957
age	652	big	158	church	925	difference	542	experiment	737
ago	449	bill	506	circle	498	different	171	explain	464
agreed	930	birds	312	city	217	difficult	971	express	746
ahead	915	bit	770	class	433	direct	781	eye	219
air	184	black	342	clean	768	direction	510	face	279
all	34	block	896	clear	472	discovered	573	fact	423
allow	959	blood	852	climbed	704	distance	543	factories	906
almost	284	blow	843	close	232	divided	515	factors	611
alone	739	blue	537	clothes	594	division	997	fair	912
along	230	board	816	cloud	730	do	47	fall	389
already	626	boat	456	coast	763	doctor	809	family	298
also	145	body	301	cold	381	does	153	famous	844
although	656	bones	814	color	303	doesn't	974	far	281
always	241	book	269	column	923	dog	310	farm	376
am	482	born	917	come	96	dollars	866	farmers	512
America	198	both	243	common	462	done	401	fast	356
among	484	bottom	685	company	901	don't	227	father	212
amount	653	bought	965	compare	830	door	328	fear	960
an	43	box	408	complete	314	down	92	feel	422
and	3	boy	140	compound	818	draw	378	feeling	800
angle	680	branches	850	conditions	990	drawing	740	feet	254
animal	186	break	792	consider	858	dress	697	fell	777
another	154	bright	642	consonant	648	drive	600	felt	507
answer	192	bring	463	contain	427	drop	539	few	228
any	137	British	970	continued	707	dry	465	field	396
anything	514	broken	658	control	752	during	335	fig	948
appear	604	brother	562	cook	813	each	44	fight	690
apple	983	brought	459	cool	729	early	348	figure	394
are	15	brown	727	copy	631	ears	718	filled	476
area	308	build	669	corn	986	earth	218	finally	409
arms	561	building	431	corner	802	east	741	find	90
army	884	built	500	correct	411	easy	324	fine	496
around	146	burning	713	cost	788	eat	278	fingers	700
arrived	993	business	790	cotton	982	edge	568	finished	572
art	799	but	31	could	79	effect	998	fire	399
as	16	buy	621	couldn't	699	eggs	535	first	83
ask	165	by	29	count	672	eight	874	fish	307
at	21	call	86	country	208	either	607	fit	821
away	185	came	142	course	428	electric	803	five	361
baby	620	can	39	covered	355	elements	834	flat	838
back	112	cannot	487	cows	991	else	709	floor	617
bad	735	can't	501	create	969	end	152	flow	795
ball	492	capital	905	cried	382	energy	517	flowers	595
bank	764	captain	780	crops	805	engine	738	fly	406
base	448	car	255	cross	601	England	712	follow	141
be	22	care	616	crowd	831	English	402	food	204
bear	677	carefully	437	current	890	enjoy	833	foot	716
beat	694	carry	266	cut	290	enough	277	for	13
beautiful	565	case	635	dance	524	entered	862	force	458
became	415	cat	673	dark	491	entire	985	forest	549

Alphabetical Order: FOR-REA

farm	147	history	787	lay	582	molecules	920	pair	497
forward	955	hit	807	lead	643	moment	659	paper	244
found	193	hold	358	learn	196	money	374	paragraph	589
four	265	hole	687	least	702	months	588	park	891
fraction	681	home	172	leave	297	moon	520	part	99
France	921	hope	633	led	966	more	72	particular	887
free	632	horse	311	left	226	morning	363	party	759
French	692	hot	479	legs	551	most	114	passed	364
fresh	937	hours	341	length	557	mother	191	past	569
friends	323	house	187	less	446	mountain	289	pattern	369
from	25	how	48	let	285	mouth	747	pay	742
front	421	however	339	let's	689	move	174	people	80
fruit	863	huge	950	letter	190	movement	847	per	657
full	478	human	798	level	918	much	130	perhaps	505
fun	856	hundred	367	lie	853	music	302	period	765
game	457	hunting	794	life	240	must	157	person	414
garden	773	I	20	lifted	882	my	81	phrase	628
gas	711	ice	608	light	220	name	121	picked	526
gave	407	idea	276	like	65	nation	637	picture	178
general	516	if	50	line	132	natural	665	piece	319
get	95	I'll	392	list	294	near	202	place	108
girl	287	important	250	listen	351	necessary	879	plains	710
give	113	in	6	little	105	need	169	plan	383
glass	579	inches	424	live	110	never	215	plane	451
go	74	include	499	located	994	new	101	planets	872
God	779	increase	786	long	91	next	235	plant	209
gold	662	Indian	282	look	70	night	257	play	182
gone	577	indicate	835	lost	731	no	77	please	774
good	121	industry	894	lot	666	nor	980	plural	928
got	246	information	745	loud	857	north	372	poem	832
government	475	insects	804	love	531	northern	968	point	188
grass	719	inside	439	low	340	nose	943	pole	848
great	126	instead	627	machine	447	not	32	poor	688
Greek	963	instruments	585	made	97	note	434	position	861
green	442	interest	560	main	553	nothing	435	possible	661
grew	721	interesting	840	major	876	notice	384	pounds	655
ground	388	into	67	make	64	noun	485	power	486
group	247	iron	698	man	123	now	89	practice	753
grow	262	is	7	many	56	number	76	prepared	934
guess	826	island	444	map	375	numeral	370	present	564
gun	951	isn't	909	march	967	object	481	president	726
had	28	it	10	mark	309	observe	877	pretty	935
hair	651	it's	299	match	972	ocean	432	printed	913
half	404	itself	708	material	493	of	2	probably	550
hand	177	Japanese	870	matter	502	off	181	problem	313
happened	344	job	567	may	98	office	949	process	883
happy	575	joined	715	maybe	789	often	248	produce	430
hard	236	jumped	613	me	111	oh	412	products	343
has	69	just	119	mean	135	oil	88	property	886
hat	885	keep	213	measure	346	old	136	provide	810
have	24	kept	559	meat	881	on	14	pulled	377
he	11	key	725	meet	586	once	268	pushed	619
head	222	killed	683	melody	684	one	27	put	151
hear	270	kind	176	members	525	only	104	questions	306
heard	325	king	390	men	167	open	237	quickly	413
heart	544	knew	316	metal	605	opposite	931	quiet	664
heat	477	know	107	method	645	or	26	quite	638
heavy	495	known	443	middle	670	order	326	race	563
held	598	lady	796	might	231	other	53	radio	902
help	128	lake	647	mile	256	our	118	rain	533
her	62	land	170	milk	663	out	55	raised	590
here	163	language	467	million	580	outside	623	ran	454
high	200	large	156	mind	530	over	100	rather	829
hill	618	last	210	mine	819	own	206	reached	350
him	66	late	274	minutes	417	oxygen	927	read	168
himself	359	laughed	636	miss	275	page	189	ready	513
his	18	law	717	modern	817	paint	529	real	283

Alphabetical Order: REA-YOU

reason	558	sharp	900	stick	758	thousands	470	watch	280
received	772	she	46	still	195	three	148	water	84
record	571	ship	332	stone	667	through	129	waves	349
red	327	shoes	941	stood	450	thus	811	way	78
region	521	shop	938	stop	271	tied	864	we	36
remain	696	short	336	store	566	time	68	wear	734
remember	347	should	197	story	224	tiny	660	weather	583
repeated	922	shoulder	893	straight	755	to	5	week	445
report	754	shouted	706	strange	775	today	334	weight	880
represent	591	show	144	stream	871	together	245	well	155
rest	436	shown	416	street	425	told	320	we'll	903
result	612	side	253	stretched	956	tone	806	went	166
return	522	sight	868	string	842	too	134	were	35
rhythm	873	sign	570	strong	418	took	263	west	581
rich	865	silent	827	students	797	tools	989	western	924
ride	615	similar	952	study	194	top	331	what	33
right	133	simple	527	subject	518	total	976	wheels	440
ring	782	since	317	substances	987	touch	744	when	37
rise	756	sing	386	such	160	toward	360	where	127
river	264	single	743	suddenly	508	town	391	whether	593
road	403	sir	995	suffix	939	track	992	which	45
rock	353	sister	926	sugar	946	trade	828	while	229
rolled	676	sit	545	suggested	859	train	536	white	259
room	315	six	489	sum	546	travel	397	who	87
root	584	size	490	summer	547	tree	214	whole	345
rope	981	skin	722	sun	305	triangle	919	whose	771
rose	958	sky	578	supply	801	trip	686	why	164
round	455	sleep	609	suppose	761	trouble	728	wide	555
row	701	slowly	373	sure	329	truck	911	wife	899
rule	483	small	149	surface	429	true	366	wild	574
run	249	smell	988	surprise	691	try	175	will	51
safe	824	smiled	679	swim	888	tube	878	win	973
said	40	snow	614	syllables	504	turn	162	wind	352
sail	675	so	60	symbols	733	two	71	window	541
same	138	soft	592	system	452	type	639	wings	846
sand	808	soil	629	table	371	uncle	793	winter	554
sat	552	soldiers	825	tail	815	under	223	wire	766
save	736	solution	936	take	103	underline	999	wish	538
saw	225	solve	603	talk	292	understand	460	with	17
say	125	some	61	tall	625	unit	393	within	649
scale	654	someone	674	teacher	597	until	251	without	272
school	211	something	233	team	778	up	52	woman	762
science	875	sometimes	288	tell	139	upon	400	women	964
scientists	438	son	606	temperature	641	us	173	wonder	678
score	954	song	295	ten	405	use	42	won't	812
sea	260	soon	293	terms	889	usually	321	wood	398
seat	996	sound	102	test	509	valley	723	word	30
second	273	south	385	than	82	value	845	work	106
section	646	southern	910	that	9	various	929	workers	961
see	75	space	354	the	1	verb	419	world	199
seeds	760	speak	602	their	49	very	115	would	63
seem	234	special	494	them	58	view	1000	wouldn't	914
seen	380	speed	671	themselves	640	village	610	write	73
sell	892	spell	183	then	57	visit	769	written	556
send	867	spot	854	there	41	voice	379	wrong	932
sense	841	spread	897	these	59	vowel	365	wrote	705
sent	732	spring	634	they	19	wait	410	yard	748
sentence	122	square	503	thick	851	walk	258	year	109
separate	791	stand	304	thin	860	wall	548	yellow	908
serve	783	stars	420	thing	117	want	143	yes	471
set	150	start	216	think	124	war	387	yet	474
settled	907	state	267	third	587	warm	461	you	8
seven	839	statement	757	this	23	was	12	young	291
several	357	stay	441	those	242	wash	895	your	38
shall	596	steel	975	though	466	Washington	962	you're	720
shape	468	step	362	thought	221	wasn't	820	yourself	751